DINOSAUR COLORING BOOK FOR KIDS

- RUSS FOCUS -

ISBN-13: 978-1721064397   ISBN-10: 1721064397
PUBLISHED BY RUSS FOCUS COPYRIGHT © 2018 ALL RIGHTS RESERVED
NO PART OF THIS PUBLICATION MAY BE REPRODUCED IN ANY
FORM OR BY ANY MEANS WITHOUT WRITTEN PERMISSION OF THE PUBLISHER.
WE ARE NOT RESPONSIBLE FOR UNSOLICITES MATERIAL PUBLISHED IN USA

SAMPLE
DINOSAUR
COLORING
17 of 41
PAGES

www.russfocus.com

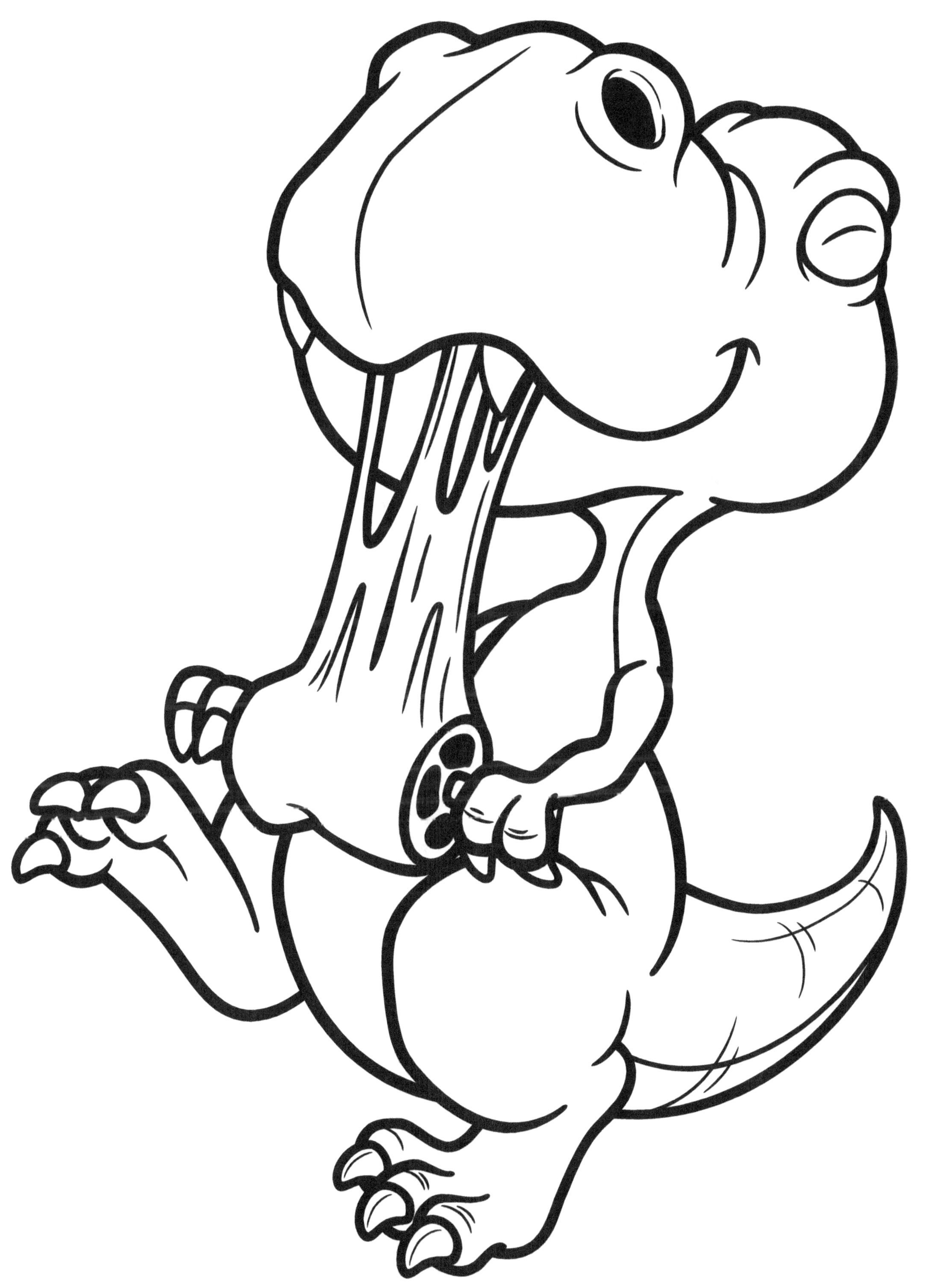

www.ingramcontent.com/pod-product-compliance
Lightning Source LLC
Chambersburg PA
CBHW080033260726

48658CB00007B/2587

* 9 7 8 1 7 2 1 0 6 4 3 9 7 *